NLP

Learn Neuro Linguistic Programming And Develop A
Powerful Mindset To Achieve Your Goals In
Relationships And Life

*(Establish A Constructive Mental Environment That Will
Have An Effect On Your World)*

OtmarHeigl

TABLE OF CONTENT

Then, What Exactly Does Critical Thinking Entail?..................1

Get Ready With All Of Your Financial Documentation...........19

Create An Atmosphere Of Panic, Then Attempt To Calm It........27

The Best Workout For Shedding Pounds..........32

Put The Target In Perspective 44

The Extraordinary Effectiveness Of Reciting The Gayatri Mantra....................62

Pretend That You Completely Anticipate To Get More Than What You Are Requesting And Act Accordingly....................75

Imagine The Alteration............................83

Why Being Organized Is Essential To Your Creative Success.......................101

Learn How To Read Body Language – Examples Of Poor Body Language.........................129

Utilizing The Knowledge That You Have Obtained 146

The Fact That Others Control And Dominate Them Is The Utmost Reality Of The Situation 153

Then, What Exactly Does Critical Thinking Entail?

You would suppose that the first thing that they have learnt in jail is that they should have resisted the desire to use social media straight after they had done something bad. This is one of the lessons that they have learned in prison. On the other hand, you may be startled to learn that individuals often make the most irrational choices. Some individuals engage in criminal activity for no other reason than the thrill of the act. In addition to that, there are things known as crimes of passion, which occur when a person's thinking becomes confused by their emotions.

There are also some who have the tendency to believe that simply because they have had success with something, it should be possible to replicate that success for everyone else. In Atlanta, there was this cult that held the belief that gazing directly at the sun would clear one's mind, despite the fact that ophthalmologists would disagree with this viewpoint. There is also the possibility that you are acquainted with a man who would advise you to treat a health problem by consuming something repulsive and unprescribed by a medical professional. To this you would presumably respond by assuming that it is impossible to consume anything unclean while also curing an illness.

And then there are some individuals who, in their haste to reach a conclusion, are prone to making mistakes in their calculations of the potential outcomes, thus putting both their convenience and their resources at jeopardy. What is it that they do not have? Thinking critically is essential, of course.

Analysis and Reflection To define it:

People are capable of evaluating the truth of a proposition and coming to a choice or conclusion about it based on that evaluation. The process of utilisingone's reasoning to determine if something is true and how one ought to behave in various situations is an example of the critical thinking process. In the same vein, the manner in which you evaluate the reasonableness of your actions and choices is also a component of it.

When seen in this context, critical thinking might be understood as "thinking about thinking." It is the process of carefully examining one's own ideas in order to determine whether or not such thoughts really make sense. Because one's actions originate from their ideas, having the ability to think critically enables one to choose rational actions when the option of acting on what they believe to be reasonable is being considered.

Why Is It Necessary for You to Study It?

You may be convinced that you will not be doing anything even somewhat intelligent in this lifetime; yet, you must acknowledge that there are occasions when you make mistakes of judgement owing to your emotions or some erroneous ideas that you have. That would make you human, but a sensible human being would want to make as few mistakes in judgement as possible in order to experience life to its fullest to the extent that it is feasible.

It is a well-established truth that gaining knowledge of critical thinking may significantly improve one's intelligence. Although it will not make you more intelligent in a certain academic field, it will make you more intelligent overall. To begin, it enables you to make more effective judgements, such as selecting the appropriate item while you are shopping. Additionally, it enables you to make more significant decisions on a global scale, such as determining whether or not you should be thinking about human rights.

You Should Get Familiar With the Fundamentals First.

You should be acquainted with the following three terms if you want to continue reading, since you will be exposed to them in the next paragraphs. These three things are called a claim, an issue, and an argument.

What exactly is a "Claim"?

A claim, often known as a statement, is the assertion of the truth or falsity of something. As an illustration, the statement "Fluffy is a cat" is an example of a claim. Now, it is the responsibility of every critical thinker to investigate whether or not that assertion is genuine. If you are familiar with Fluffy and know that he is a dog, then you are aware that this assertion is not true.

Claims need to be looked into since doing so will lead to the uncovering of the truth about the world that you are a part of. It is essential for you to determine whether or not the programme that you purchased the previous week is, in fact, compatible with your computer, exactly as the salesperson promised. At the same time, it is of the utmost importance to determine whether or not members of Congress are stealing your taxes. You may improve the quality of the judgements you make by doing research on the statements that you hear and see in the world around you.

Be mindful, however, that not all assertions need investigation since they are either demonstrably true or demonstrably false. There are a lot of assertions, though, that need a more in-depth investigation on your part since they would force you to make really significant choices about your life. As a result of this, you have an obligation to be aware of the claims for which a greater degree of scrutiny is warranted.

What exactly is the problem?

You are bringing up an issue when you call into doubt the veracity of a claim. That entails the fact that this concept is already a question in and of itself. To put it another way, if you want to express your disagreement with anything that you have read or heard, you should pose a question about it, which will turn it into a problem.

Although it may seem straightforward at first glance, there are several circumstances in which this assumption is not valid. The reason for this is because there is a strong possibility that you are not addressing the appropriate problem here. You could even find yourself in a situation in which you are unsure whether or not you want to create an issue out of a claim since you do not even know what the claim is aiming to. This might be one of those situations.

Also, here is something else that you need to be critical about: there are some lines or words that are out there that are not assertions, but they are there to make sure that you, as the listener, get confused, or just unchallengeable. So be critical about that. Either they make no sense at all, or there is no way to determine whether or not they are true or untrue since there is no way to test them. Either way, it is impossible to investigate them. The issue that arises now is whether or not you ought to give consideration to those items.

When it comes to determining what you should make a big deal out of, your beliefs, values, and the experiences you've had in the past will all come into play. For instance, if someone tells you that "God is dead," you technically do not have any proof, either scientific or physical, to establish that this is not the case. But if the teachings of the religion that you hold in high regard tell you differently, then you have every right to make it your mission to debunk what they say.

What exactly is an argument, then?

Arguments are the most essential component of critical thinking due to the fact that this is the stage at which one weighs the reasons why one believes or does not believe a claim, as well as the reasons why one should create an issue out of it. When you stop and give it some thought, you may see that you have been in a debate ever since you started to pay attention to the allegation, whether you supported it or questioned it.

Critical thinkers are aware that arguments are constructed in such a manner that individuals may have means of judging the validity of everything that takes place in the world. In the vast majority of cases, there is a good chance that you will not even know whether you were successful in making the ideal argument in demonstrating that a claim is true or not. Your line of reasoning, on the other hand, is the one that will be taken into consideration.

You should now have a fundamental understanding of how critical thinking works. In the next chapter, you are going to learn how critical thinking has truly transformed the world throughout the course of history.

Principal Components

Being organised does not need a lot of effort. It does call for a certain amount of perseverance, time, honesty, bravery, and desire. Because it may be an endeavour that lasts a lifetime, you should get started as soon as possible.

The ideal strategy for the majority of individuals is to start off on a modest scale. Pick an activity that piques your interest and put in the effort to make it a regular part of your routine. Now we may proceed to add the next component to the puzzle. It is up to you to choose what strategies are successful for you.

After a certain amount of time has passed, you will eventually have developed some confidence and momentum. Now would be a good moment to go back, get a fresh piece of paper, and decide out how you want to go about approaching each day from the ground up. Keep in mind that you should employ the components that you have discovered to function for you.

Establish Your Priorities

If you don't know what matters most to you, it will be impossible for you to effectively manage your time, energy, and attention. Because of this, you really must make advantage of the discovery phase.

The next thing to do is to decide on three top priorities for the coming year. This would be split down into objectives for the next three months, one month, one week, and one day. This ensures that you will begin each day with a clear understanding of the tasks that are most important to you. It's possible that you'll need to adjust them as a result of things that take place in your life, but doing so will be a deliberate decision on your part.

It is quite beneficial to do this every day. It's possible that when you first start doing this, it may seem theoretical, but when you've made it a habit, it will all of a sudden make perfect sense.

Boost Your Concentration and Energy Levels

Because you can't create more time, you need to locate activities that can boost your concentration and energy levels. Some examples of these might include when and what you eat, hobbies, meditation, relaxing, resting, and exercising.

Include them in your routines every day if it is something that is essential to you. They will increase the efficiency of what you do.

Regular Activities

It will require some work to establish new habits and get started on new projects, but sustaining such changes won't be as challenging. The most important thing is to establish certain habits that will be beneficial to you. Make an effort to get your priorities straight, ask yourself the same questions in the evening and the morning, and mentally plan out how you want your days to go. You need to make sure that you are sticking to the habits for focusing, relaxing, eating, and exercising that work best for you.

After you have created these routines, they will not need as much of your time or energy, and you will have the flexibility to spend the bulk of your attention, energy, and time on things that are vital at that particular point in time.

The use of Timeboxes and Hotspots

Every hour is different from the next. There will be parts of the day in which you are able to successfully do challenging activities. There are going to be instances when you are unable to. There are some periods of the day in which you shouldn't be working at all, so take those times off. It is helpful to determine the times of day when you are most productive and to make sure that you devote this time to tasks that are challenging, time-sensitive, or significant. If you need to hold a meeting at a time when you aren't at your best, plan an agenda and practise when you are at your best. This will help you perform better when the meeting actually occurs.

It would be helpful if you could allocate enough time to the primary responsibilities. Put less important activities on life support by denying them a lot of your time. Whatever you can get done in that amount of time will be sufficient.

Questions Upon Questions

Your thoughts and feelings will be guided by the quality of the questions you ask. Your actions will be influenced by these factors as well. You should always maintain a list of questions ready to ask in response to different scenarios that may arise. Take, for instance:

What behaviours are you going to give up? Is it possible to outsource or subcontract the task?

What are you willing to settle for? It's possible that you don't want to, but you have to.

What will you continue to uphold?

What are some things you're going to start doing or do more of?

Will it be beneficial to take these steps? Are you able to devote the necessary amount of time or effort to affect change?

Are you really doing something or are you simply keeping yourself busy?

Do you have three goals that you want to accomplish today?

Do you have three goals that you want to accomplish this week?

Do you have three goals that you want to accomplish this month?

Do you have three goals that you want to accomplish in the next year?

Where do you plan on going?

Is there anything you can do to provide a hand?

Do you have any recommendations for me?

Start, occasionally pick up the Pace, but Always Cross the Finish Line

You will need to choose when you will start and when you will end. Begin from square one. It is OK to start again if you discover that your beginning is not as you imagined it should be. There are several benefits associated with sprinting. You must complete whatever it is you're working on and find a means to do it. Be careful to close any open loops that you find.

Creating a Setting From Scratch

It is critical to surround yourself with individuals who will stimulate your creativity, keep you energised and on track, and help you maintain your concentration. Your working environment may have a similar effect on you; for example, the images on the walls, the colour of the walls, the reminders that are around you, and even the state of your workspace in terms of its cleanliness can either propel you ahead or hold you back.

You may also keep yourself on track by surrounding yourself with positive affirmations and positioning them such that they draw your attention.

Choose carefully the individuals you work with and the setting in which you do your job, if at all possible.

Get Ready With All Of Your Financial Documentation.

When making a strategy for your budget, the first step you need to do is to collect the necessary evidence. Put on your finest sleuth hat and acquire as many financial records as you can possible get your hands on. This will help you figure out what's going on. This is very important since these papers will provide you with a distinct understanding of the money that is entering and exiting your wallet at any one time. Which specific papers should you be searching for at this time? In a nutshell, anything that displays a monetary sum in written form, in whatever form it may take. The following are some examples:

receipts of payment bank statements

accounting for investments

bills for credit cards, utilities, receipts for loans, and accounts of other loans

You have most likely grasped the concept by now. You should always be prepared in case you come across a document that might serve as evidence of a financial contract or transaction that you have previously entered into and that you have made. It cannot be skipped since it is the very first and most important phase in the process. It is a given that there is a possibility that you will be unable to get a hold of certain receipts or utility bills from the weeks or months prior to the ones in question. That's not a problem. Simply collect as much as you possibly can. The further you go, the more reliable the information you uncover about your company's finances will be.

Determine how much money you make per month.

After that, you need to figure out your average monthly income. If you were successful in applying all that you learned in the previous chapter, you would have a number of different revenue streams at your disposal. Because of this, it could be difficult for you to keep track of the amount of money that is flowing into your life and precisely where it is coming from. On the other hand, if you maintain a record of everything via your bank accounts and receipts, then the procedure should be pretty straightforward for you. The most important thing for you to do right now is to calculate your typical monthly income. It is likely that the quantity of money coming in will change from one month to the next if you have alternate sources of income in addition to your primary source of revenue, which is your day job. That's not a problem. You are not need to provide an exact quantity. What you need is an average monthly income that can serve as a dependable baseline for you to construct the remainder of your budget plan around. You can calculate this income by multiplying your current expenses by 12. The amount of money you have available to work with on a monthly basis is the central focus of every subsequent phase in the process of developing a budget plan for your household.

Notes of significance:

You are allowed to include government assistance, such as Social Security or child support payments, in your income calculations.

If the amount of money you make from various side gigs is too unpredictable and fluctuating from one month to the next, you should choose the month in which you made the least amount of money and use it as a baseline. When you design your financial plan in this manner, you are adopting a more responsible approach.

Prepare a Breakdown of Your Monthly Expenses

After you have determined how much money you bring in each month, the next step is to break down all of the money you spend each month into individual categories. Make careful to write down everything that you do while doing so. Take a mental note of the amount of additional gratuity that you gave to a waiter or waitress the one time that you ate out. If you parked your car somewhere and paid a charge, it counts as a cost as well. People, in most cases, will only concentrate on their most significant expenditures, such as their monthly payments and other such things. Nevertheless, over time, even the smallest of things may add up to a significant amount. For this reason, it is essential that you itemise each and every one of your costs, regardless of how large or how little they may be.

If you are having difficulties remembering how you have been spending your money, then all of the receipts and billing statements that you have been keeping are there to help you do just that. If you choose to do most of your shopping online, all of your transactions will either be stored on the online stores you frequent or sent to you through email. You need to make sure that no stone is left unturned in order to have a decent understanding of the amount of money that you are spending each and every month. The following are some red flags to watch out for:

repayment of loans and mortgages

the costs of insurance premiums

bills for food purchased outside the home and travel

parking fees as well as personal maintenance costs (such as visits to the barber and the doctor)

Expenses associated with travel, such as petrol and train tickets, among others.

billable services

Create An Atmosphere Of Panic, Then Attempt To Calm It

The employment of fear as a tool for social control is now popular as well as very successful. Fear has the ability to effortlessly affect and control people, regardless of whether or not they are motivated by their emotions or their rationality. The key to effectively dealing with fear is to first make someone afraid, then to provide them a way to calm their nerves. This strategy is fantastic for making money off of things, disseminating knowledge (via channels such as the media), and achieving nearly any other goal you could have.

This strategy consists of a clear two-step process: first, instill dread in the other person about something, and then provide them with a remedy that causes them to feel relieved. In order to get the most out of this strategy, you need first have a rough notion of what you may utilise to instill terror in your target audience. In other words, you will need to do an appropriate analysis of the individual in order to have a clear picture of the things that they could be terrified of. Then you may make advantage of this to organically instill terror in others. After you've accomplished this, you want the answer you provide to be one that provides some kind of relief.

The following is an example of creating dread followed by delivering relief:

The following has been reported in the news: "Today, sixteen persons have perished as a result of an attack by an unknown source. The police have not been able to identify the suspect despite the fact that several witnesses have said that they are aware of who carried out the assault. In the meanwhile, twenty-three more people are now being treated in the hospital for injuries ranging from small scrapes to significant damage caused by the bullets that were shooting through the crowd. These injuries were caused by the bullets that were pouring through the crowd.

Stay tuned, as we will keep you informed with new facts as the situation develops.

Every day, we are presented with several sorts of manipulation, such as the one described above. In light of the fact that many individuals have been shot and the perpetrator is still at large, we are understandably terrified. In a strict sense, the relief would come from the police, who are now conducting a search for the person who attacked.

However, the news broadcaster has transferred the relief to be the news station itself since they are claiming to be the ones who will supply us with live updates and alert us when the assailant is ultimately apprehended. This movement in responsibility comes as a result of the news broadcaster's shift in responsibility for the relief.

Therefore, the public relies on that news presenter for respite from the terror rather than on the government, who are the traditional source of such consolation.

The objective is to position your business as the provider of true anxiety reduction through the use of your product, service, offer, or solution. When individuals are scared, they often want nothing more than for their fears to go away and for them to experience a sense of security and ease once again.

You are the one who orchestrates both halves of the approach if you are the one who can first induce dread (without making it appear like it was done on purpose) and then deliver comfort (without making it look like it was staged). This implies that you can swiftly "sell" your solution since the person you are speaking with is actively "buying."

The Best Workout For Shedding Pounds

Let's be honest: the only reason you don't exercise is because you're too lazy to do it! There are a lot of individuals who claim that they do not have enough money to visit a gym or purchase fitness equipment. But you don't need any money at all to do straightforward workouts like sit-ups, push-ups, and running. Another common complaint is that individuals just do not have enough spare time. However, you do have the opportunity to read this book. Let's be honest with each other: you are too lazy to work out.

If you are one of those individuals who, when they hear the word "exercise," immediately provide excuses such as "Do not have the time," "Do not have the money," or "Exercise will make me unable to focus on work," then I will suggest a straightforward kind of exercise that you may do: walking.

Do not undervalue walking just because it is something that we do often. It has been shown that walking may assist a great number of individuals in achieving their optimum weight. It is because they move about a lot and include walking into their daily activities if you have ever wondered why individuals who never exercise, who never go to the gym, yet nevertheless have a beautiful looking physique. If you have ever wondered this, the answer is that they move a lot. They burn calories by walking around. The fact that we walk on a daily basis is the primary reason why we do not consider walking to be a kind of exercise.

Walking is an inexpensive, basic, and straightforward form of exercise. Walking is a less expensive form of exercise as compared to joining a gym, taking dance lessons, or enrolling in swimming classes. Walking is one of those activities that puts almost all of the body's joints to work. Your arms, legs, and back all move at the same time when you do this exercise. Walking is the greatest activity for burning extra calories and maintaining a healthy weight since it keeps you moving.

One of the methods to speed up your metabolism is to go for a walk. Walking raises the pace at which your body burns calories, which means that you will almost certainly see some weight loss as a result. When you begin to walk, you will immediately begin to burn calories. Even if you just walk for two miles, it will boost your metabolism for up to twelve hours after you finish.

Many different health programmes have consistently recommended that we begin walking at least 10,000 steps every day. You can keep track of your steps using a pedometer. Ten thousand steps are a lot less than you would imagine they are. Your daily aim should be to walk 10,000 steps, which is equivalent to around 5 kilometres.

The act of walking may be done almost anyplace. There are many different things you may do to walk more. You have the option to walk to the workplace, and you also have the option to wake up early and walk there. If your workplace is too far away, you may park a little farther away and start walking in that direction instead of driving. You may increase the amount of walking you do by engaging in a variety of activities. Some of these activities include using the stairs instead of the lift or escalator, parking farther away from the entrance of the workplace or mall, cleaning out the office desk or even walking around a boss while watching a movie.

Walking for exercise and weight loss is hard effort. However, if you merely exercise and do not make any changes to the way that you eat, you will not see a significant improvement. When you combine regular walking with eating in a way that is both healthy and nutritious, you will not see rapid weight loss.

Always keep in mind that altering your lifestyle and developing new routines is necessary in order to achieve your weight loss goals. What is the purpose of doing a lot of exercise if you are going to stop after you have achieved your desired body composition? You will eventually get your fat back. Walk more if you want to keep your weight the same without having to do strenuous workout! Maintain your regularity, and you will start to notice the benefits.

4) The deceitful manipulator wants you to believe that they are the epitome of perfection in every way. They are not pleased with the fact that you are acquiring their behaviours and beliefs via the use of NLP. Because their haughty attitudes need them to continually seek for self-affirmation, they will not cease casting a net for praises from you in order to confirm the inflated notion of themselves that they have in their heads. Because a person who is mentally sound would never engage in behaviour like this, this is often the first sign that you are dealing with a person who is not who they claim to be. If someone has this personality and then learns NLP, they might be extremely hazardous for someone else who is unaware of NLP. This is because the person's ability to easily influence and convince others just validates the person's already inflated impression of who they are as a person to someone who is unaware of NLP. You should give serious consideration to breaking off communication with someone who is

demonstrating these narcissistic qualities, particularly when they are attempting to use psychological manipulation on you. This is not an easy thing to convince yourself to do, but it is in your best interest. Although having psychic resistance will get you far, it does not imply that you should continue to spend time with those who have it.

5) The dishonest manipulator believes they are deserving of having everything handed to them on a silver platter. It will not be enough for them to obtain what they want if they can just succeed in convincing everyone else to give up what they are doing. The malevolent manipulator views the fact that they do not already have everything and everyone exactly the way they want it to be as a significant offence at all times. Because of this, they have a very short temper with other people, and as a result, you may discover that you are the only one who decides to continue spending time with them. It is in your best interest to follow the example set

by everyone else in their life and get away from them.

6) A wicked manipulator will never feel guilty or ashamed about their actions. It is natural for a manipulator who does not want to do harm to others to have these feelings from time to time. It is healthy for us to examine what we are doing and think about whether or not we are moving in the correct direction. At the very least, so long as we are not physically close to the issue at hand, it is not inappropriate for us to reflect on what we are doing and to examine the morality of what we are doing. However, a wicked manipulator would never act in this way. They do not experience these feelings because, in their thinking, it is inconceivable that they could be responsible for anything. Therefore, they do not believe that anything could be their responsibility. The dishonest manipulator doesn't even consider the potential that they may do anything that would be considered unethical. The unfortunate reality is that the fact that

they can shape individuals via the use of psychology and NLP makes them even more assured of this. It's possible that at the beginning of your encounters with them, you, too, had this impression of them. However, it never lasts for very long, and eventually you begin to recognise them for who and what they really are.

You should pay attention to these warning indicators not just in yourself but also in other individuals in your life. Using the information and abilities you have just gained, you will want to be absolutely certain that you do not take advantage of other people in an unethical manner. If you already know that you would never intentionally do damage to another person via the use of psychological manipulation, then you should be particularly cautious to look out for these indicators while interacting with other people. A very moral person like yourself might be quite vulnerable to being influenced by these dishonest people without even realising that they are doing so. You should place a particular emphasis on developing your psychological resilience.

If you ever find yourself tempted to utilise the information included on these pages for the objectives described above, you should keep in mind that there are an infinite number of options available to you besides doing so. Whatever you decide to do with the information is entirely up to you, but be assured that there is much to do even without the use of NLP in a setting like this one.

When someone seems resistant to making changes in their life, you might utiliseneurolinguistic programming (NLP) to encourage them to take action. You may even utilise it in a manner that will exclusively benefit you, while preventing any other person from being harmed in the process. Remember this when you go on to the next chapter and study the ins and outs of influence, since none of these situations will cause you to behave in a way that is indicative of someone who is intentionally trying to manipulate others.

Put The Target In Perspective

The target must be broken down as the last phase in covert manipulation. You have reached the stage when you know the other person as intimately as you possibly can. You are aware of what makes their mind tick, as well as their anxieties and strengths, and you have a broad understanding of who they are. After that, you are prepared to start damaging their sense of self-worth in some manner. Imagine their self-esteem to be their armour; the stronger it is, the less likely it is that you will be able to influence them by installing your strings and getting them to do what you want. Destroying someone's sense of self-worth is a certain way to turn them into an easy target for exploitation. When this occurs, it is less likely that he or she would reject the manipulation or stand up to any abusive behaviours that are being carried out. It is more likely that he or she will come to trust your own judgement, which will result in him or her losing the confidence in his or her own actions that would have enabled her to effectively challenge you.

Keep in mind that this will take some time. If you begin by becoming too large too fast, the target audience will realise what's happening and depart. Think of this like getting used to being around water. If you want to take a hot shower, you should begin with the water at a temperature that you can stand, and then gradually work your way up to temperatures that, if you had gone right into them, would have been so uncomfortable that you would have leapt out of the shower to get away from them. If you try to make too great of an impact too early, your target is going to run away from you.

You may begin with jokes that aren't too obvious, such as something that you can honestly refute. For instance, if you want your girlfriend to lose weight and you want to push her into doing so, you may make a joke about pregnant ladies immediately after prodding her stomach. It's possible that the comment made her feel a little insecure, but if she brings it up with you, you can just shrug it off and tell her that she must have been imagining the connection between the comment and the touch. You can also tell her that she shouldn't be so sensitive, or that if she is that sensitive, maybe she should take action instead of just moaning about it.

This might then be taken one step further; the next time your girlfriend orders a meal that is unhealthy or wants a snack that is high in fat or sugar, you may raise an eyebrow, almost in a disgusted manner, and question her choices without really saying anything to her. She may then call you out on it as well, to which you should again deny, stating that you never glanced at her like way. She may then call you out on both of these things. In a tone that conveys mild disapproval, gently remind her that you do not have authority over her bodily functions or the food or drink that she chooses to consume. You may progressively chip away at her sense of self-worth without having to do anything extra by taking advantage of the fact that she is probably feeling uneasy about herself at this moment in time. Even if you do not care about her weight, criticising her looks is one of the simplest ways to pick at someone else. People are often most concerned about their own appearances, even if their appearances are good to begin with.

In addition to this, the next time she chooses something unhealthy at a restaurant, you should be somewhat more overt, such as sighing in disdain. This will show her that you are not pleased with her choice. You continue to reject the behaviour as being linked when questioned about it, rather than blaming it on a difficult day at work or anything else that is not relevant to the situation. You want her to feel uneasy about herself to the point where she immediately draws inferences, and you also want her to feel insecure to the point where she doesn't believe her gut response when you do something that is purposely designed to make her feel insecure.

The last step in further demeaning her and breaking her self-esteem would be to actually say anything, since this would be the stage that would involve speaking something. You may make a remark about how she often complains about her weight, but she never does anything to address it, and how it is obvious that she does not care about the additional weight that she carries since she has never made an attempt to get it off by exercising or dieting. This last phase is likely to do significantly more damage than the others did, but the purpose of the whole process is to gradually reduce her sense of self-worth until it is nonexistent. When it is at zero, you can start putting her back together again, which includes attaching all of the strings and buttons that she needs to have in order for you to be able to completely control and operate her yourself. Once it is at zero, the process is complete.

Your girlfriend is not likely to connect you to any changes in personality that may be seen. This is because the shifts in personality have been occurring gradually over such a long period of time, and you have repeatedly denied any participation with the unpleasant remarks or filthy glances. It's possible that she'll come to the conclusion that she needs to reduce her weight. She is also likely to be much more receptive when you exhibit subtle symptoms of disapproval, which is something else you should keep in mind. Even the tiniest smirk or scowl, even if it is just for a split second, will be sufficient to instantaneously provoke that insecurity in your partner, enabling you to superimpose your own wishes and beliefs in place of her natural response.

There are instances when people refuse to believe you or us. These metaphors and short tales were produced with the intention of assisting those who are experiencing difficulties in life, as well as providing therapists with fresh perspectives on the subject.

We are about to embark on an adventure that will take us both to infinity and beyond. Some people consider your ideas to be as meaningless as the electrical discharges that occur constantly in your brain. To others, though, they are an integral component of the way life is constructed. Nothing more than substance and the void in between, webs are nothing more than that. It is my hope that you will discover the missing component that has eluded those who can only locate the gaps.

You are going to discover something in this book that you are going to want to carry with you for the rest of your life, no matter what.

You could discover that the tales plant the seed for some personal development that you want to pursue. They will provide you with some kind of explanation. Always keep in mind that I am not giving you something that you did not already have; all I am doing is providing the tools for you to locate it.

Please make sure that everyone who is in need of assistance hears that notion.

DECOMBINATION OF AIR

For effective stress alleviation, having a basic understanding of relaxation is essential.

Terry and his wife Juliet travelled to a little town in France and leased a gite there. They were finally going on the summer vacation of their dreams and had been looking forward to it for a long time. Their lives were fraught with tension. They put forth a lot of effort, yet there was always more work for them to do. They were under an incredible amount of strain from their employment. The expectations that were placed on their time were like weights that needed to be borne like burdens. Their lives were like balloons that had been blown up too much and were about to pop.

During the day, the sun shined, and during the night, the stars sent forth a radiance. When the sky was clear, there would be shooting stars that would race through the night.

They would both yell, "Make a wish!" every time.

They would consider their own ideas while keeping their eyes closed. Nobody will ever know the secret of what you desire for when you wish upon a star.

During their stay together of two weeks, Pierre was a neighbour. Aside from being able to place an order for a cup of coffee, a beer, or a glass of wine at a restaurant using their limited French language skills, he could not speak any English.

They didn't care much about the outcome since they were more concerned about being together and away from anything that may add further stress and anxiety to their life.

They were looking forward to a meal, some wine, and some downtime.

Pierre saw that his temporary neighbours were having a good time during their vacation.

One day, when he gazed over the garden wall, he said the phrase "Décompressez." He beamed as he pointed and grinned at the mansion.

Terry's concern stemmed from the fact that the petrol tank located in the lawn required some maintenance. He conducted an investigation and examined anything that had the potential to trigger an explosion. He came up with nothing.

In his garden, Pierre was taking care of the veggies he had grown.

Terry yelled out in French, "Bonjour." The salutation was reciprocated, and Pierre nodded in acknowledgement.

"What exactly is it that needs to be decompressed?"

The word "Décompressez" was Pierre's response, and he smiled as he walked away.

Terry felt certain that this guy knew more than he was willing to let on about at this point in time.

"What exactly do you mean when you say 'decompress'? What exactly needs to have its pressure reduced? If I don't do it, what will happen to blow up?"

Pierre called out "Attendez" before turning and walking away.

Terry, who was more concerned than he had been previously, shared with Juliet that the "tonday" required decompressing, irrespective of what and where that entailed.

They could hear laughing emanating from inside Pierre's home.

"French to the bone!" Terry's mutterings were more irate.

A young woman, maybe in her twenties, could be heard laughing as she emerged from the residence of Pierre.

"How are you today, sir? I am the grandson or granddaughter of Pierre. I am able to communicate with you in English because to the lessons that I have taken." Her accent was interesting, and her voice was soothing. Terry's anxiety began to subside.

"According to my grandpa, whenever he advises you to relax, you seem to experience a heightened state of anxiety. There is no need for alarm at this time. He suggests that you and your wife seem to be having issues, and that you should use this opportunity to rest and unwind while you are on vacation. Decompress is the term that he loves to use the most.

Permit the tensions you're feeling to be released into the fresh air. Isn't it a better termthan'relax'? It is possible for a word to lose its meaning if it is used excessively, as is the case with the term "relax." How exactly do you relax, and how does it make you feel? It is not an easy task. When you hear the phrase "decompress," it brings a deeper meaning and a more concrete image to your mind. My grandfather wants you to have a good time in this place you call home and apologises if he ever caused you any anxiety.

There is one more thing; would you be available for supper this evening at seven o'clock? I will be present to provide translation services. By the way, it is part of my work. I am employed in the UK.

They responded well to the invitation.

"We are now beginning the decompression phase of our mission." They agreed with each other in tone.

By the way, looking at a female while protruding your tongue is not an acceptable form of decompression. Juliet commented on this with a grin not just on her face but also in her voice.

And with that, the decompression process got underway. They were able to unwind since they lacked a sense of direction. They may take the meaning of decompressing, of letting the tensions go, to unwind, to loosen up, and to calm down rather than sitting in the shade of an umbrella and trying to plan their peacefulness by urging themselves to be peaceful. This would allow them to plan their peacefulness more effectively.

"You know, when I saw the shooting star, one of the things I longed for was the capacity to relax because I wanted to plan it like I do at work. One of the things I wished for was the ability to rest. I purposely made it a difficult objective that required a lot of work to accomplish. The process is clear to me now. Never fear, all of that pent-up negativity will be released all on its own if you just let it. Simply allowing the tumult of life to calm down into a soothing breeze is what this is all about. It seems that my wish has been granted.

"The same goes for me," she said. remarked the other participant.

The Extraordinary Effectiveness Of Reciting The Gayatri Mantra

There is a narrative told in Zen about a wretched guy who, while wandering in the woods, ruminates about all of his problems. He came to a halt and rested against a tree, an enchanted tree that had the power to fulfil the desires of anyone came into touch with it as soon as they did. He was aware that he was thirsty and desired something to drink. Instantaneously, a glass of ice-cold water was handed to him. Astonished, he took a look at the water, evaluated it, and then made the decision to drink it. After then, he became aware that he was hungry and expressed his need to have something to eat in his possession. He suddenly had a supper in front of him. He couldn't believe it when he realised that his desires were coming true. He said the following words aloud: "Well, then I wish for a beautiful home of my own," The house suddenly materialised on the field in front of him. His face broke out in a broad grin as he expressed his desire for staff to look after the home. When they arrived, he recognised that he had been mysteriously gifted with an enormous ability, and he desired that he might share his good fortune with a lady who was beautiful, loving, and intellectual. The guy turned to the lady and said, "Wait a minute, this is ridiculous." "I'm not quite as fortunate as you. Nothing like that could ever happen to me. As he spoke...everything vanished before my very eyes. He gave a shake of the head and said, "I knew it," before turning and walking away while ruminating on all of his problems.

This seemingly straightforward Zen tale really conceals a profound insight. The human mind is comparable to this enchanted tree. Whatever the mind can conceive of and believe, it will ultimately do. Our rishis have known and comprehended this timeless principle even since the time of the Vedas. The repetition of mantras is one of the techniques that may be used to reprogram our subconscious thoughts. Mantras, unfortunately, are much like the mystical tree that was described in the Zen tale that was just told. Those who have faith in the power of mantras might benefit from using them. Mantras are a potent tool, and the Vedas, Upanishads, and Samhitas are all excellent sources for them. The Gayatri Mantra is considered to be the most important of all of these many mantras. The Gayatri Mantra is considered to be the most important of all the Vedic mantras since it has been chanted by Indian rishis over the years and because it is given the most prominent position. "Among the Mantras, I am Gayatri," Sri Krishna proclaims in the Holy Geeta. Sri Krishna is a godhead of the highest rank.

The renowned Gayatri Mantra is said as follows in its Vedika form: Om bhur-bhuvah-svah tat saviturvarenyambhargodevasyadhimahi dhiyoyo nah pracodayat

Om! is one possible translation for this phrase. Let us ponder the divine energy that permeates the land, the atmosphere, and the heavens. That may serve to orient our thoughts. This mantra is spoken during the day's three transitional points, sometimes known as twilights, and Savitur is the name of the sun.

The tantric collection known as the Prapanchasaratantra provides a very detailed explanation of the Gayatri pujas and meditations. This article explains how the mantra Om hums in the Muladhara chakra, which is located at the chakra's base, and how it ascends via seven levels to reach the crown chakra, which is located at the top of the head. Known as the Sahasrara.

According to the teachings of our sages, Mahavishnu explains Om as being composed of the following: Bhuh is existence, Bhuva is the elements, Svah is the atma of everything, Maha is magnificence and light, Tat is Brahman (the absolute), Tapah is all knowledge, and Satyam is supremacy and interior understanding. This tantra establishes a connection between the three letters of Om (A, U, and M) and the seven other realms. (For further information, see also the JnanasankaliniTantra.)

Tat is an ultimate Brahman and refers to the original source of all the matter in the universe. It is represented as fire in the circle of the sun. Savitur is the origin of all that breathes and lives. Varenyam is regarded as the most worthy, and hence gets devotion. Dhimahi is a term that alludes to wisdom being golden and constantly being inside the sun. Bharga is a term that indicates it removes sin, and Devasya implies it is full of light. Dhiyo is another name for Buddhi, while Yo is another name for energy (tejas). The mantra may be broken down into three portions consisting of eight letters each and four sections consisting of six letters each. A dhyana, also known as meditation, explains that Gayatri has three faces: a white face, a crimson face, and a black face. (morning, afternoon, and evening; visually, aurally, and kinesthetically).

In spite of this, the tantrik tradition offers fresh perspectives on the Gayatri. For instance, the text known as the Matrikabhedatantra has a couplet that states a yogi is someone who has knowledge of Brahman, also known as the absolute. In the tantrik tradition, every facet of a devata is associated with a particular version of the Gayatri mantra, and this mantra is often said at various points during the day, including midnight.

For instance, one of the lines from the TripurasundariGayatri reads as follows: "Tripurasundarividmahe, kameshvaridhimahi, tannoklinnepracodayat."

This phrase translates as: Let us think of Tripurasundari, let us think of Kameshvari, and may that sweetness guide us.

As a kind of visualisation, the GandharvaTantra employs all 24 possible syllables of this mantra in Sanskrit, beginning at the bottom of the spine and working its way up to the crown of the head. The mantra known as Ajapa is the name of the other tantrikGayatri. As a person breathes in and out over the course of a day, this mantra is inadvertently repeated several hundred times by that person. One half comes from the sun, while the other comes from the moon. Only the letters Ha and Sa make up this symbol. Gayatri is said to assume the shape of Brahma in the morning, the form of Vishnu in the afternoon, and the form of Shiva in the evening. According to the ZeNLP taxonomy of visuals, auditories, and kinesthetics, the recitation of the Gayatri Mantra may be found on the following page:

• Visuals, which should be recited first thing in the morning, then Chakra Meditation should be done.

- Recitations in the afternoon, followed by sound vibration, are to be considered auditories.

- Kinesthetics is a recitation to be done in the evening, to be followed by dynamic meditation.

This ZeNLP categorization is based on the mental map that you choose as your favourite. Therefore, if you want to get the most out of reciting the Gayatri Mantra, you need to figure out which mental map works best for you before you start reciting it. After that, you may reap the advantages of the Gayatri Mantra. Because of the importance of correctly pronouncing the Gayatri Mantra at the beginning of this sacred recitation, you should seek the assistance of a knowledgeable guide. During ZeNLP seminars, participants are supplied with this professional advise, which is based on the participant's chosen mental map.

There are several different variations of the Gayatri Mantra, the most well-known of which are the Agni Gayatri, the VarunaGayatri, and the PruthviGayatri. It is advised that kinesthetics recite 108 repetitions of Agni Gayatri at dark, while visuals should chant 108 times of VarunaGayatri at midday. Chanting these mantras in a scientific manner is a speedier way to awaken the universal awareness.

God is the source of all life, the brightness of the world, the unending beginning and the one who sustains the process of the universe's creative cycle. Being the source of all life on earth, the sun is often used as a symbol for God because of its role as a creative force. The Vedas are the poetic expressions of God spoken in a metalanguage. This metalanguage is the sound correspondence of the omniscience and boundless creative delight of divinity, the might of infinity, and the majesty of immortality. Savitur is considered to be a representation of the divine inside the Vedas. On the level of eternity, Savitur is synonymous with God. On the plane of the physical world, it refers to the sun. On the plane of the mental, it denotes intellect. On the plane of the biological, it denotes vitality. The Gayatri Mantra may be found in the Yajur Veda (36.3), and it is considered to be the core of the Vedas.

In point of fact, the Gayatri is a classic expression of the blazing omniscience of Divinity that is condensed into only 24 words. It is a sign of the brilliance of the Divine pulsating through the earth, heaven, and the places in between, inspiring life with energy, intellect, and blissful pleasure. It is an ode to the sun, which represents the sublime. As Lord Krishna explained to Arjuna in the Bhagavad Gita, the splendour of Lord Savitur, the Creator sun, is comparable to the cosmic explosion of a thousand suns breaking out on the horizon on the first dawn of the Universe. This is a revelation that was made by Lord Krishna to Arjuna.

The Gayatri Mantra has the power to elevate our souls to a higher level of superconsciousness via the effect of its beauty, wonder, and happiness. It puts us in a state of prayer that prepares us to take part in the creative ephiphany of the Universal Mother. In a world that might otherwise be shook by death and agony, it throws open the floodgates of light, bringing with it the beatitude of serenity and immortality.

Mantras, kalmas, and psalms are all forms of potent autosuggestion that are used to train the unconscious mind. Managers might profit from being aware of this fact. These auto-suggestions may be made to sink into the unconscious mind more quickly by recognising the chosen mental map and programming it in the proper manner. Considering that each manager has a unique method for programming his unconscious mind, this is possible. It is possible for managers to become subconsciously competent in attaining their objectives by allowing strong affirmations relating to personal and organisational goals to sink into the unconscious. To put it another way, it improves their efficiency and effectiveness and makes it possible for them to accomplish their objectives by taking the route that presents the fewest obstacles. Unconscious competence gives managers the ability to optimise outcomes while minimising the amount of effort used. This involves reducing risks as much as possible while simultaneously increasing potential profits. In the parlance of business, unconscious competence assures the most possible profit with the fewest possible expenses. In a spiritual context, the word "unconscious competence" refers to the act of tapping into the strength of the infinite intellect that is within oneself in order to accomplish one's objectives.

A student of martial arts approached his instructor with sincerity and said, "I am committed to studying your martial system." How much longer will it take me to get the hang of it? The educator answered in a nonchalant manner, "10 years." The student's response, which was marked by impatience, was, "But I want to master it faster than that." I intend to put in a lot of effort. If it is necessary, I will practise every day for at least ten hours each day. In such case, how much longer will it take? The instructor pondered the question for a time before responding, "20 years."

Pretend That You Completely Anticipate To Get More Than What You Are Requesting And Act Accordingly.

Obviously, this is based on the assumption that you are aware of not just what you want but also what you are willing to accept as an alternative. People have two different sorts of expectations in every form of transaction: what they would prefer, and what they would be willing to settle for. What I observe time and time again is that individuals wind up with precisely what they would consider to be satisfactory as a compromise. That teaches us a very valuable lesson, doesn't it?

Quite a few years ago, I had the opportunity to collaborate with several consultants who were just starting out in the industry of providing consulting services. The consultants were required to conduct sales calls and to inquire about possible clients' availability for meetings. One young woman said that she was having difficulties with this and that she was unable to get people to participate in meetings, despite the fact that she was normally successful in convincing them to receive brochures.

Consider the concept of modelling strategies: if the outcome is repeatable, there must be a process operating in the background.

I inquired as to what she hoped to accomplish, and she said, "Well, what I would really like is to get a meeting." Subsequently, I inquired as to what she would consider an acceptable alternative, and she responded, "Well, I would be happy if they let me send them a brochure."

Because people have a tendency to do precisely what they set out to do, it is important to double verify the results even if they do not match your expectations.

Making preparations for your approach

You need to have a strategy in place before you can put any plan into action. To put it another way, after you have settled on what it is that you desire, the next stage is to take some action. What is the question, exactly?

The act of planning a strategy is not the same as really carrying out the plan. In the end, in order for others to give you what you want, they need to be aware that you want it. As a result, the following is the second key to successful negotiation and influence:

Asking for what you need or desire is the quickest and simplest approach to receive what you need or want.

And make sure you are being as straightforward as you can. There is no guarantee that other people will comprehend hints and mild nudges, or indirect requests, or any of the various ways that we make ourselves feel less self conscious about communicating our wants. You cannot rely on other people to grasp these things. If you do not make it a practise of telling others what you want, you have no right to expect that they would give it to you.

Do you remember what we mentioned about expressing what it is that you desire?

"What I need from you is... How do you feel about that?" "What I want is..." "What I need from you is..."

Gaining an understanding of both requirements and results

If you want to assist other people achieve what they want, one of the most crucial skills you can have is the ability to comprehend other people's wants, even if those other individuals aren't particularly good at articulating those demands. Think back to a moment when you had outstanding service at a store or restaurant; I'm willing to bet that it was because the other person anticipated your requirements or went above and beyond what you anticipated they would accomplish.

It is simple to assume that you are surpassing the expectations of your clients when you provide them with more than they have requested; nevertheless, you should take care not to provide them with "more" according to your standards rather than to theirs.

When it comes to hiring a removal company to assist me in moving home, for instance, price is not the primary selection consideration that I utilise if it falls within a generally competitive range. My primary considerations are dependability and caution; I need the moving firm to arrive when they say they will, work quickly, and take care not to damage anything. In order to get something, I am willing to pay more than the cheapest price provided that it is "in the ball park," which means that it is within the range that is determined by the supplier's rivals or the market.

If a removal firm wants to obtain my business, they will undoubtedly be eliminated from consideration if they give me a discount. If a firm provided me with a list of prior clients that I could contact, it would definitely increase my level of satisfaction, but I doubt that I would make contact with any of them. If the representative of the firm who arrives to make the estimate exudes an aura of self-assurance and competence, there is a good chance that I will go with that particular business.

Therefore, in order to meet and surpass the expectations of your clients, it is essential to have a solid understanding of their criteria and the ways in which these criteria vary from your own.

In the process of negotiating, everyone wants something in order to acquire something else; for example, people want automobiles so they can travel places, furniture so they have somewhere to sit, and money so they can purchase things. The objectives of the negotiation are not the goal of the negotiation; rather, they are a means to an end. Find out what aims are being served by the negotiation, since this will be a very helpful step for you to take in the discussion. You will become more adaptable and productive as a result of this.

The one and only occasion I've ever seen really dissatisfied consumers was when they were provided with the item(s) they requested rather than the item(s) they desired. Therefore, you should never merely give people what they ask for; instead, make it a habit to find out what it is they really want.

Although it may seem to be self-explanatory, a surprising number of salespeople are unable to determine the needs and desires of their clients. Your proficiency in NLP should make this an easy task for you to complete.

Imagine The Alteration.

We have read quite a few times that change is the only thing that is constant in life, and it is true that if you want to be successful in life, you will require a significant amount of change in both your brain process and your imagination. I am going to show you how to transform your negative thoughts and pictures into good ones in the next chapter of this book.

I have previously stated this concept in the chapter that came before this one: the mental image that you create triggers a chain reaction consisting of ideas, inward dialogue, and feelings, which all culminate in the behaviour that you exhibit. If the first step of this procedure is a good thinking, then the outcome will also be positive; however, if the first step of this process is a negative idea, then the outcome will also be negative. The majority of the time, individuals are concerned by something in their lives that makes it harder for them to go through difficult moments when they arise. The mental image that was created in their minds is the explanation for it. There are always two perspectives that one may use when looking at a circumstance. The first one is considered to be negative, whereas the second one is considered to be positive. In most cases, people go with the first choice rather than the second one, which is something that really shouldn't be the case. That is something that we can work on together to improve.

An illustration of what goes on in the Picture Works factory that is our mind is shown below, and I will explain how I want you to transform the unfavourable image into a favourable one.

Negative Picture Works Factory Problem: I am going through a lot of financial trouble right now.

Image Constructed: Whenever I try to picture the situation, all that comes to mind is me losing all of my money. I am unable to pay the bills or return the debts since I do not have any money. Because I am now unable to pay the rent, I anticipate being asked to quit the apartment in the near future.

Conversation with oneself: I can't believe I put myself into this mess! I simply don't have it in me to do anything worthwhile in this life. I despise what I do for a living. Some people seem to go through life with ease. Why should not I? My problems seem to have no solution, and I am becoming more frustrated by this situation. No longer can I continue living like way. I want to expire soon. I absolutely despise the way my life is!

Feelings and emotions include being upset, worn out, stressed, having an inferiority complex, feeling looser, hopeless, furious, fed up, and considering ending one's life. My whole body hurts, is stiff, exhausted, and stressed out, and it has a weak feeling.

Action: I will go to my supervisor and ask for an advance on my paycheck so that I can pay the bills for the time being. I am not sure how much longer I will be able to keep up with this. If nothing changes for the better in my life, I shall just take my own life.

Isn't this how you often get yourself caught in the hamster wheel of pessimism, which then leads to you making poor choices? This is not the way you should be thinking at all, it is incorrect, and you need to rethink how you are thinking about this. Imagine for a moment if everything at your Picture Works Factory was operating on a happy note. Permit me to demonstrate it to you.

Are you interested in learning how to manipulate people? Being manipulative and gaining talents in the art of manipulation

The term "manipulators" refers to covert bullies who take use of their power over others in order to profit themselves, advance their careers, get benefits, or even avoid getting a job. They are all proficient in the arts of concealment, seduction, and deceit, which is the one thing they share in common. Because of this, they are very dangerous and exceedingly poisonous creatures. Because of this, a number of research have concentrated on gaining a better understanding of the behaviours of these individuals as well as the methods they employ to deceive others. Because of them, we now know that they often engage in behaviours that are very similar to one another. Being aware that it is without a doubt essential:

In general, every single one of the most skilled manipulators is also an adept in the craft of seduction. They have realisedthat feigning care for the requirements and preferences of others is an efficient and speedy approach to acquire influence over those around them. I see, that is how they operate. Praise without measure and support for individuals who are designed to attract him are two of his go-to strategies for winning people over. They will be able to earn their confidence in this manner, which will result in their demands being granted without condition.

The exceptional oratory ability of these individuals is unmistakably one of the defining characteristics of the group as a whole. Con artists hone all of these skills to their very maximum potential. And the pinnacle of their skill is getting their victims to give in to their whims, persuading them of the compelling reasons that justify their acts and that they do not want to take advantage of them, even if it means that they are injured in the process. They never fail to make a reference, within the framework of their strategy, to the importance of justice, solidarity, or the common good. Despite this, they often leave out the fact that they are the ones who stand to gain.

They are masters at playing the part of the victim, and they are well aware that doing so is a highly successful strategy for convincing others to give in to their demands. In the words of the trickster, there are many references that are designed to make people unhappy. For example, the trickster may say things like, "I don't want to do this," "I'm having a very hard time asking you to do it," or "I suffer for all those who have a bad time."

They often volunteer to act as the group's representative when asked about it. Therefore, many people disguise their own egotistical motivations and a desire for power beneath the facade of working for the benefit of others. They often beg for our cooperation in applying for a job or offer to talk with our supervisors on our behalf. Watch out for those who say they can save us. It's possible that your aims aren't really admirable. They nearly always want something in return, whether it is votes, money, or labour of some kind. Dictators, politicians, leaders of cults, televangelists, and visionaries all fall under this category. They all use strategies that are quite similar to one another, yet we don't improve.

The amazing capacity of professional manipulators to induce feelings of guilt in other people is without a doubt one of the skills that they cultivate to a greater extent than any other quality. They are aware that individuals who are more aware of and sensitive to the feelings of others are more likely to submit when they are made to feel guilty. They chose them as victims because they are more susceptible, and this is why they choose them. It is sufficient to imply that they are required to prevent damage, and they will say things like, "If I don't finish the job, they will fire me." in order to deceive people into believing that they are required. They will instantly feel sorry for you and offer to assist you.

Putting the blame on their victims will distract from their real goal, which is to advance themselves financially. They have thus become skilled at giving persuasive arguments in order to induce feelings of guilt in people who suspect them. They often respond with questions such as "Who? Me?" or statements along the lines of "I don't know how you think that, after what I've done for you." "I have nothing but good intentions. I dare you to provide evidence to the contrary." They are aware of the difficulty. It is a strategy that is incredibly successful.

They resort to sneaky methods of intimidating others. It has been shown that the vocabulary of these individuals is often riddled with indirect threats, threats that are implicit, or threats that are subtle. They will make statements such as, "I understand that you don't do anything, but this will kill us," "if you don't invest, you will lose all of your money," or "if we don't intervene, we risk an atomic war." One of the most common strategies used by these covert aggressors is to instill terror in their targets.

At other instances, they use veiled mockery in order to sow seeds of doubt. Creating a sense of uneasiness in other people is an efficient strategy for gaining influence over them. "Who, among them, will rescue us? It is imperative that we take action.

It is standard practise to neutralise the victim by persuading him that others look down on him and treat him poorly in order to make him feel powerless. This will make it much simpler to persuade him to give all of the responsibility to the con artist: "I know it's unfair. If you would like, I may make a statement on your behalf.

One of the most common strategies employed by this kind of covert aggressor is to place blame on other parties. They are skilled in the art of locating scapegoats, and at times they do it in a covert manner. On other occasions. Every day, politics teaches us something new about how to make good use of this instrument.

They are sometimes accused of or blamed for the activities they have taken. As a result, it is quite typical for individuals to "play dumb" in order to excuse their disregard for the requirements and emotions of others. They often apologise by saying something along the lines of "I'm sorry, I didn't realise that this could affect you."

If you ask them questions that are plainly worded, they will demonstrate that they are pros at shifting the topic and evading difficult queries. We need to keep this in mind in order to identify a con artist.

In conclusion, it has been shown, as was to be anticipated, that they have a high propensity for lying, virtually always doing it by omission. They don't generally invent tales, but when they do, they twist important parts of the truth or just forget about such parts. They are easy to spot because they respond in a roundabout manner and employ the body language of people who are trying to conceal something, particularly when they are confronted with inquiries that are straightforward.

By the way, we may continue to be amazed by the mysterious impact that some individuals have on the lives of others. They like complex and understated methods of seduction the majority of the time, although this is not always the case.

It is a fact, however, that none of this has been able to stop future elections from taking place. It is possible for the influence of some individuals to completely eradicate one's capacity for thought, at least in a critical sense.

How is it doing with the handlers?

Therefore, the manipulators are able to obtain control by discovering a reward from their victim and then calculating how much that reward will benefit them. The purpose of this article is to identify manipulative mindsets and provide ways to combat them.

1. They are experts at identifying the areas of vulnerability in other people.

The manipulative person will try to find out what your weaknesses are, and if the chance presents itself, they will use them against you. For example, if you have any doubts about what you believe or if there is something that makes you feel ashamed and you want to hide it, the manipulative person will try to find out about these things, and if the chance presents itself, they will use it in you against you.

2. They won't give up until they have accomplished what they set out to do.

They don't seem to mind treading on anyone's toes at all. They believe that the aim justifies any methods used to get there. They do not experience any tremors when they are about to act in order to carry out the steps required to accomplish what they have set out to do. since of all this, their actions are almost never called into question since they are such skilled performers.

3. They are unable to be satisfied

They get a sense of power from manipulating others, and as is often the case with those who have power, they want more of it. They are aware that by alone, they are unable to achieve a goal, but that their talent for manipulation may enable them to achieve their objective by making use of the merits of others behind their backs. As a result, their moral values have been partly compromised as a result of this awareness. They are driven by their ambition, a desire that, similar to the effects of narcotics, may lead to a kind of addiction.

4. They need a sense of mastery

It is common for the manipulator to have what is known as a superiority complex. Manipulators are often persons who have characteristics that are similar to egocentrism and narcissism. They like pushing themselves to better and go beyond the level they have already achieved in order to take on more difficult tasks.

Nevertheless, persons who feel the need to believe themselves better than other people, or even flawless beings, and who benefit off the accomplishments of others, imply a certain insecurity that they cover up with the impression of authority. Nevertheless, a crippling anxiety lies dormant inside that deep part. to give the impression of weakness.

As a result of the fact that manipulation is an art form, we can state that those who are gifted in manipulation possess a variety of talents and capabilities. Within this category, there are many subtypes of manipulators, each of which will be discussed in more detail below.

Conclusion

> *Thank you again for downloading this book!*

In this book you have learned all there is to know about the wonderful process of self-hypnosis that will ensure that your life is changed for the better. We have started by taking a look at the wonderful benefits that are afforded by this ancient process, before we have moved onto the actual techniques that we need to inculcate in order to actually make it happen.

We have then seen all the pivotal tips that we need to bear in mind, in order to make that self-hypnosis session every bit of the grand success that it deserves to be. We have also seen the cardinal things that we need to avoid, if we need to firmly ensure that our self-hypnosis efforts are not wasted.

By now you must be probably raring to go where it comes to using the powerful tools of self-hypnosis as a means to change your life for the better, right? Of course you are. The best part is, you have gotten all the ingredients to make that hypnotic session of yours a great success, thanks to this book.

So, go on out there and conquer the world by using the magic that is called self-hypnosis. You will marvel at the change that will occur in your life and those self-hypnosis sessions of yours will become an addiction for you – well, at least an addiction that is healthy for you. It is truly an addiction that will conquer any negative ones and fill your life with positivity.

Finally, if you enjoyed this book, then I'd like to ask you for a favor, would you be kind enough to leave a review for this book on Amazon? It'd be greatly appreciated!

Why Being Organized Is Essential To Your Creative Success

There are a lot of individuals who try to hide behind the idea that creative chaos may lead to significant accomplishments. However, if you are interested enough in the idea to conduct any study on it, you will discover that it does not relate to your day-to-day existence. It pertains to a global structure of a pattern that is far bigger than what your mind can see and envisage, which means that what appears to be an unorganised and chaotic pattern right now is really a fantastic design that will emerge at some point in the future.

When it comes to human life, chaos is exactly what it sounds like: a condition of complete disarray and confusion that can only result in greater disorder and confusion. Let's see how well the idea works out in the real world. Your desk is piled high with papers, documents, pens, erasers, and perhaps even the book you're currently reading that's peeking out from beneath some newspaper that's been there for a week. If a colleague calls and asks for a paper, you start hunting for it on your desk, inside your drawers, and ultimately end up printing it out simply to avoid having to sift through the mess. You did not take the time to make several folders on your internet browser in order to keep the various kinds of bookmarks organised; therefore, you are forced to attempt to remember the names of the websites in order to look for them in your history. The content of your email is a different story. You may search for all emails that include a certain term by just typing it into the search box and seeing them all display. On the other hand, there were instances when searching for a particular message may take more than an hour. The search for a file on the computer is an adventure best left to the bravest people who also happen to have a lot of spare time on their hands.

The sole result of all this commotion is increased anxiety and headaches. You may be able to persuade yourself at the moment that you are in command of your time and space, and that you have everything you need at your disposal and in a place where you can easily see it. When you take everything into account, you will see that you spend one hour every day hunting for various things. That amounts to a minimum of five hours every week. Remember that these routines will eventually seep into your private life as well. You do the same thing in your kitchen, closet, and hallway, and we are all aware that you have a chair that is specifically made to retain all of the clothing that you changed many times during the day or week. In addition, tasks such as paying bills, making appointments, and planning activities for your leisure time are put off until the very last possible minute. It's no surprise that you're so busy.

The ability to recognise and create patterns is one of the hallmarks of the human species. If the way in which our nature was made had been different, ancient man would have died out a long time ago. Our modern lives have given us modern difficulties, despite the fact that we no longer live in caves and do not kill wild animals for sustenance. In today's world, if you keep your surroundings crowded and you let time slip by without making the effort to efficiently manage it, you will throw off the balance between your personal and professional lives. This equilibrium has to be maintained in its current state. In the alternative, you put yourself at risk for illnesses associated to stress, failures in your work life, and a lot of restrictions in your personal life. Therefore, if you have a habit of letting the cards fall where they may, it is probably time to break that pattern and develop a new one. one in which you are in command of and in control of your life and the time that you spend.

The First Precept: Mutual Obligation

When one person makes a gesture towards another, that other person automatically feels obligated to reciprocate the action. One good illustration of this practise is provided by the Hare Krishnas, who will present the recipient with a flower or a book and then, as soon as the "gift" is acknowledged, ask for a payment.

If you donate something to another person and they say "thank you" and you respond with "It was nothing" or something similar, you are unintentionally diminishing the favour they have given you, and as a result, they feel as if they have no obligation to you in return. You may reply something along the lines of "I know you would do the same for me." You reply in a kind manner and leave them with the impression that they owe you something by providing a place for them to communicate with you.

Commitment and stability are the focus of the second principle.

When a plan is committed to, whether verbally or in writing, there is a greater chance that the plan will be carried through. Even when there is no motive or incentive to do so, or even if the motivation or incentive is withdrawn after the agreement, the rationale for the commitment is that it is compatible with the self-image.

In the 1960s, researchers pretended to be volunteer workers in order to carry out an experiment in which they urged homeowners to construct a huge, unsightly fence on their property that bore the words "Drive carefully." Naturally, almost no one was interested in doing this, and as a direct consequence, just 17% of the property owners agreed to the request. The rate increased from 17% to 76% when a seemingly insignificant change was made. How was that accomplishment made? You will observe.

A couple of weeks ago, the detectives requested that the owners show a modest notice measuring three inches that stated "Be a Safe Driver." Considering how minor this proposal was, practically everyone gave their assent to it. Nevertheless, the owners were more open to putting up the bigger sign when another volunteer visited a couple of weeks later than they had been before. Why, after they accepted to post the modest notice, did they feel the need to also consent to put the other enormous one that was so invasive of their property?

because they feel the need to maintain coherence throughout their whole lives.

Because of this, when you want to leverage this concept to your advantage, you need first have one individual do something modest to build the tiny commitment, and then they will definitely remain committed for larger demands.

The third principle is that of social proof.

Imagine this: you are going on a vacation, and while you are there, you come across a spot that has two restaurants, one of which is packed with vehicles, and the other of which is almost vacant. Which restaurant do you choose to go to? The full house is completed by nine out of ten players. You will not go "despite" the fact that it is full; rather, you will go "because" it is full. It is possible that they believe that since they are already full, the meal will be of a higher quality. This is an example of social proof.

For this reason, you will see marketing methods that state something along the lines of "Join the more than 500,000 members already active" or something like. Because of this, it is one of the most effective strategies of persuasion, and you may utilise it by displaying views, testimonials, and examples of individuals who put what you teach into practise. You may utilise it to establish agreement; for instance, if practically everyone agrees with something, then those who are less certain are more inclined to accept it since it is the view of the majority. You can exploit this to your advantage by using it.

The Fourth Principle: Authority

People have a tendency to follow those in positions of power, even when they are asked to do things that are dubious or immoral. The Milgran experiment is a good illustration of this point. Participants were instructed to "electrocute" actors who acted as though they were going through the condition. This was done by a group of researchers. The participants were unaware that there were not, in fact, any electric shocks and that there was merely a show. Even though they cried and begged him to stop, the actors continued to electrocute the victims, despite the fact that the victims were pleading for compassion. This was owing to the immense power that the authorities has.

Another experiment that was conducted was one that was intended to be funny. A sign was affixed to an automated teller machine that stated "Out of service, turn over your deposits to the policeman." The experiment was conducted by a journalist who posed as a law enforcement officer and wore a badge, outfit, and even a baton while conducting the test. Within the span of only two hours, the journalist was successful in amassing a total of $10,000 in cash and cheques. Not counting the bank data that customers supplied him, which included secret codes and social security numbers among other information.

When the journalist revealed his true identity, he questioned the individuals about why they had agreed to the request, and they said that it was because of the outfit. Remember that having authority is much more than just being strong; it's also about how you come across to others.

Even though you won't likely be dressed up as a law enforcement officer, you can still demonstrate your authority by displaying strong body language and speaking in a tone that is forceful, resonant, and authoritative.

The fifth persuasive principle is that people are more easily swayed by individuals that they admire. At one point in time, a collection of different merchants was investigated. Those who formed a "relationship" with consumers, engaged in conversation with them, listened to what they had to say, and learned something about the other person's life were more successful at selling products than those who just knocked on more doors; even those who did so had a lower number of successful sales.

That is the influence that one's taste may have. People are more likely to bargain with people they have a positive relationship with.

The use of these principles of influence enables you to capitalise on the fundamental human needs that motivate others to take action, which, in turn, helps you influence and convince those around you.

Integration of Components

I have no doubt that you have had an event in which you divided into two separate people. If we use the example of the wake-up call from earlier, you are most likely thinking that this is simply a meaningless and insignificant matter. If something like this happens to you every day, do you not feel as if you are wasting your energy every morning?

Part Integration is a strategy that may help us find a solution to this kind of internal conflict. With the help of partial integration, we would be able to invite the parts of ourselves that are at odds with one another to talk with one another and negotiate for either integration or peace.

Integration of Components

1. Determine which components or values are involved in the process.

Take the example of getting up at a reasonable hour. According to the illustration shown before, there are two steps required. These are "wake up" and "get some rest."

2. Show how the two components fit together.

Place both hands in front of you with the palms facing upward in an open position. Ask each participant to take responsibility for one hand; for example, "Wake up" may go in the right hand, while "Get a rest" could go in the left.

3. Determine the constructive objective and the function of each component.

Pose the question to them, "What do you see as the positive intention of it?" For instance, "What kind of intentions do you have for me if you want me to get up early?" Asking "Why is it important?" once again after you have received an answer is a good idea. Do not stop asking this inquiry even after you have received an answer.

Discovering a more lofty objective is the goal of this exercise. Continue to ask questions until you hear the same response again. It demonstrates that the stated good purpose is the genuine one.

Then, pose the same question to another component, "What positive intentions of you who want me to get rest?" and "Why is it important?" You will come to see that the second section unquestionably carries forward the same constructive goals that the previous part did.

4. Remind them that they are working towards the same objective, and that because of this, there should be no need for them to compete with one another.

I take it that you and her share the same objective, right? Therefore, it would be preferable if the two of you could assist one another and bring the good intentions to fruition. It is not necessary for any of you to interrupt the other, is it not?

Hold off until you get a "Yes" response. If you carry out these instructions correctly, you will notice that both of your hands will be quite near to one another and may even come into contact with one another at some point.

When this occurs, you should experience a feeling of oneness in your hands and bring them closer. If you get them close enough to your chest, you may even be able to glue them together.

5. Submit a suggestion for consideration.

Make it clear to both groups that they need to work together to achieve the goal. Specify the time period, for instance one week; if it does not work, then they will bargain once again to figure out the other possible options.

6. The schedule for the future.

Imagine that you have travelled into the future to a point when there was a battle. Take note of the distinction!

Examples of Quantifiers all, each, every, some, many, none, and all are all examples of quantifiers.

Quantifiers, as the name suggests, provide a rough estimate of the quantity of something; yet, the listeners are expected to draw their own conclusions about the precise amount. Quantifiers rely on presumptions because they provide the impression that the object in question already exists.

The following are some instances of this:

1.) Because it is crafted from genuine wood, my product is a favourite of many of my clients.

Take note of how the emphasis is placed on X (Constructed of genuine wood) rather than "my clients."

Therefore, the audience's unconscious mind is leading them to believe that this nebulous "group of customers" is a valid assumption. In other words, those who read or listen to what you have to say will unconsciously agree that you have a substantial number of customers. The fact that our subconcious minds always seem to come up with something that has significance to us is one of the reasons why quantifiers are so effective. The audience often imagines that your client base is comprised of individuals who are similar to themselves, which is precisely what you want to happen.

2.) My product is so versatile that some of my clients even use it to adorn their coffee tables.

3.) Each and every one of my clients has discovered a wide variety of applications for my product.

4.) Some of my clients haven't been able to come up with several applications for my product.

The fact that this illustration is in the negative makes it more difficult to understand. This is a really captivating phrase that will simply get stuck in the reader's head straight away. The statement assumes that there is a vast consumer base, and that the audience would envisage all of the many ways in which your product may be used in addition to its primary and most apparent use. Because of this, each individual will picture something unique, something that is beneficial and significant to them specifically. This gives the idea a great deal of strength. Just right!

Assuming There Is Some Form Of Social Proof

Providing your audience with evidence from other people's experiences is an excellent method to support the message that you are attempting to convey to them. People strive to be accepted by their peers and despise the feeling of being social outcasts. They are afraid to be the first ones to do anything, but if they see that others have previously done it, they are much more inclined to act on it themselves!

An excellent method for assuming authority and social proof is as follows: (verb phrase) + which/who/that People/experts (which/who/that) (use/know) 5.) Experts who use my product express a high level of satisfaction.

Who exactly are these experts? specialists in what exactly? Everyone will conceive of anything unique in their head. Their unconscious mind will come up with something significant to them, something that will, in their opinion, make the statement qualify as being true. This will happen automatically.

6.) Customers that utilise my goods are really satisfied with it.

Take note, once again, of how ambiguous this is. Who are these individuals, exactly? Who can say?! They will fill in the blank with individuals who are similar to themselves, which is precisely what you want your audience to do. Because they will see themselves in the future as one of these "people" liking your goods, this statement is incredibly seductive.

Authorization to Take Out Loans

The practise of borrowing authority is yet another illustration of supposing the existence of social proof. In most cases, it is ideal to employ an authoritative individual or group of people who your audience is familiar with and can put their faith in. The unconsciously held beliefs of your audience will then confirm that your assertion is correct.

7.) Oak fountain pens, like the one I have, are favoured among CEOs of companies in the Fortune 500 who use fountain pens.

Take note of what you are doing here: you are establishing a connection between the notion of Fortune 500 CEOs and the product that you are selling. It will be powerful and significant to each individual, but each person will have a distinct concept of what it's like to be the CEO of a Fortune 500 company.

It is also essential to take note of the fact that you are not being dishonest. When using Hypnotic Language Patterns, we never want to be dishonest at any point. Even if you are inadvertently suggesting that CEOs of Fortune 500 companies make use of your product, you are still establishing a relationship between your product and the CEOs of those companies. You simply said that CEOs of Fortune 500 companies utilise a product similar to yours; your audience will make the connection between the two.

8.) Because hefty fountain pens are more stable, the scientists who use my pens prefer ones that are heavy like mine.

Once again, the target market will unconsciously associate your product with the nebulous category of "scientists." When your consumer buys the product, they will tell themselves that they are purchasing it because scientists utilise it. This will persuade them to make the purchase. According to them, this implies that your product must have some kind of scientific basis.

Learn How To Read Body Language – Examples Of Poor Body Language

When we mirror someone else's body language, it is essential that we fully comprehend what it is that we are reflecting. Understanding how to read people's body language is critical due to the fact that it serves as our primary mode of communication even before we utter a word. Eye contact and body language interact to establish the tone for the remainder of the discussion even before words are spoken. This is how our initial impressions of others are formed, as well as how others form their first impressions of us. Unfortunately, after these evaluations have been completed, it may be difficult to alter them so that they represent another aspect of yourself. Therefore, it is essential that you have a good understanding of how to interpret other people's body language. In the following paragraphs, we will elaborate on certain characteristics of body language:

Pointing the Finger

Imagine walking into a house where everything is disorganised and scattered all over the place. There is a general air of unhappiness with the present state of the home, and the children are not clean. In addition, there is a general air of displeasure with the children. The mother looks desperately for the television remote before furiously pointing to her oldest daughter, who is roughly 14 years old, and telling her that the issue in that home is that nobody can put anything back where it belongs. Although you are upset, your kid appears unfazed by the situation; maybe she is used to encounters of this kind.

The meaning of the message that the mother is attempting to convey is made abundantly plain by the situation that has been presented to you. Despite the fact that the whole home seemed to be in disarray, she was certain that her oldest daughter was to blame for losing the remote control. She looked everywhere for it but came up empty. On the other hand, it is not hard to miss the fact that the mother is an example of what we call a blamer. However, she was throwing all of the responsibility on her daughter despite the fact that something went wrong in the home. Because of the suggestive nature of her language, you could find yourself wondering what she means when she says to "place things back in their places" and where "around here" might be located. In a nutshell, she is attempting to convey to her kid that she is reckless and thoughtless in a way that she can understand.

There are some cues in body language that convey a sense of helplessness as well. One such example is appeasement. The act of placing one's hands at one's sides with the elbows bent and the palms facing upward is referred to as "placating." It's possible that it doesn't occur to you, but when you hold your hands in this manner, it gives the impression that you are a person who is in a position of weakness. This may or may not be intentional on your part. Because of this, you are caving in to the circumstances, and there is nothing more you can do. If you are in a position of authority in any way, shape, or form, you should steer clear of making this sort of gesture, particularly if you need to assert anything among your contemporaries.

It's interesting to note that appeasing others might occasionally work to your benefit. Take for instance the scenario in which you have a challenging message to convey. When you employ this gesture, it may provide a signal about the sort of message you wish to deliver to the person you are communicating with. Do not, however, overindulge since, in most cases, this results in an attitude of self-pity on your part.

In spite of the fact that you may anticipate a different sort of reaction when such claims are made, the daughter maintains her silence; as was said before, it is likely that she is used to this kind of conflict. Nevertheless, this is not the type of response you would anticipate in any other kind of circumstance. In point of fact, pointing fingers is considered rude in many different cultures, and when someone does so, it is the type of body language that will lead to tempers rising and harder words being used. This is due to the fact that pointing fingers at someone conveys an aggressive message and is threatening. As a result, you need to exercise caution with the way that you utilise your fingertips. If you are a parent or a teacher, or if you work with children in any other capacity, it is important that you recognise that pointing the finger at children while you are attempting to convey a lesson may have a negative impact. Because pointing fingers might be an indication that someone is being bullied, you should avoid doing it towards your spouse as well.

You have to understand that the issue with making accusations is that it is the most certain method to divert the attention of your audience away from the information that you are attempting to convey to them. Even when individuals do not talk, pointing fingers is often a reasonably accurate reflection of what they want to say and generates emotions of being frightened and bullied.

Take note that even attorneys tend to point with their fingers while they talk. On the other hand, it is quite uncommon to observe them making use of their hands. Instead, they communicate only via the use of hand gestures. If they do point, you can be sure that any of the persons being pointed at, including witnesses or even the jury, do not enjoy it. If they do point, you can be sure that any of the individuals being pointed at do not like it. This kind of behaviour in public settings like the courts can only work against you and may give the impression that you are trying to shift the responsibility onto someone other than yourself. Because it is likely to result in dispute in public and is an indication of bullying, this behaviour cannot be considered brave. On the other hand, it might indicate a lack of success, lack of confidence, or feelings of isolation on a personal level.

Clicking One's Fingers

The act of snapping one's fingers is seen to be impolite in the same way as pointing one's finger is. Imagine that someone is attempting to get your attention by making a snapping motion with their fingers. It is a terrible possibility to consider. For instance, at a restaurant, it may be extremely awkward to sit at the same table with a guy who constantly complains about inconsequential issues while simultaneously snapping his fingers to grab the attention of a passing server. This behaviour may be quite distracting. At the end of the day, they will most likely not get improved services. His lack of etiquette and disrespect for the waiter will not impress his friends, and neither will it impress the waiter. There is a good likelihood that his buddies won't sit down to dinner with him in the foreseeable future. One should not be surprised to learn that such a person is also one who points the finger and, thus, one who is quick to assign blame. Sometimes you could have the impression that these behaviours impress other people, but the truth is that the only one who is happy is you!

It's a distraction.

It is distracting when the speaker uses their arms in such a random manner that they often change the position of their hands virtually constantly while they are speaking. Although there are instances when this may seem to be without consequence, there is a possibility that it might have an effect on how others regard you, such as the public if you are a politician. When others see you, your body will appear to be tilted at an odd angle if you switch hand signals quickly. Even worse than that, it leads to misunderstanding. Because of this, the people who are listening to you won't be able to tell whether you want to remain where you are or if you are unsure. If people do not believe they can trust your intentions, it is very unlikely that they would listen to what you have to say.

The Process of TOTE

When it comes to the thinking process described in NLP, there is a pattern that the mind follows that is comparable to the structure. The approach has four parts: the Trigger, the Operation, the Test, and the Exit. It is frequently referred to as the approach that takes the route with the least amount of resistance. I'll go into more into about each of these topics in the following paragraphs:

Indicator of

The TOTE process begins with an antecedent or cue that is referred to as the trigger. This antecedent or cue is analogous to the ABC sequence of behaviour learning that I explained before. In the field of neurolinguisticprogramming (NLP), this concept is often referred to as the "Anchor," and it once again refers to the impulse or stimulus that initiates the pattern.

Effort or action

The operation, much like the ABC process before it, is related to the pattern's behavioural component as well as the cognitive habit that we carry out.

Test

On the other hand, this time the mind carries out a 'test' of the behaviour that came before it in order to determine whether or not the desired consequence was achieved. Did the individual obtain the outcome that they wanted as a consequence of taking that action? If the response is "no," then the individual will continue with the behaviour cycle until they reach the point when it is successful.

Exit

If the response to the test stage was "yes," then the next step for a person is to simply continue with their behaviour and proceed to "close the loop" on this thought pattern. This last step of completion absolutely has to take place in order to avoid going around in circles forever.

This is the normal way that we establish habits in our thinking, which can become quite strong cycles, particularly if they are constructed and strengthened over a significant amount of time. If this thought loop is really useful, then it is not necessarily a negative thing; but, if it is not, then it may be highly harmful to one's mental health and well-being. This is something that stands out pretty plainly in those who have a significant amount of obsessive compulsive tendencies (OCD).

In any event, it is essential that you try your best to end these cycles, despite the fact that it may be difficult to do so. Only then will you be able to move on from a negative cycle. Breaking destructive thinking patterns and replacing them with healthier, more constructive ones is one of the central tenets of neuro-linguistic programming (NLP). I can say without a doubt that this procedure was an essential factor in my total success. When I finally got it, I learned how to disrupt patterns.

Disruption of the Flow of Thought

The goal is to interrupt a negative thinking pattern as early on as can in the cycle or sequence, particularly between the trigger and the operation. Regardless, it has to be finished before the phase of testing the condition, which means that you need to disrupt it before the mind attempts to test the original operation pattern. If you don't, any effort to interrupt the sequence won't be very useful since the pattern is almost finished.

The pattern interruptions are not that difficult to apply, and it is just a matter of interrupting your train of thought and thinking about something new, butting in on your own thought process or dialogue that you are having inside of your own brain.

We are merely attempting to modify the course of the mind and reprogram it as we go along, just as Richard Bandler proposes. You are not so much getting rid of the old pattern as you are going around it in a different direction.

Aim high!

The goal is to make this interruption as noticeable and eye-catching as is humanly feasible. If there is one error that I see individuals making when they attempt to use this strategy, it is that their disruptive activity is too mild, and as a result, it is not sufficient to completely redirect their thoughts. In particular if it is a long-standing, deeply ingrained pattern of thinking that they are attempting to change.

Try making a really loud clap with your hands or giving a very loud cough. If the pattern that has to be broken is a negative thinking process that is related to depressed feelings, then you should attempt breaking the pattern with a small dance or jig, or by laughing at yourself. Make an effort to include humour into the disrupt since this will work entirely against the initial and undesirable behaviour and will be harmonious with the more recent and positive mind process.

Utilizing The Knowledge That You Have Obtained

It is one thing to study about NLP and learn about the things we can use to achieve success, influence people, and acquire confidence. But it is another thing entirely to put those tactics into practise. Putting the knowledge we've gained to use in our projects, irrespective of what those projects may be, is a very new ballgame altogether. Practise what you've learnt now that you've familiarised yourself with NLP and taken the time to study about the strategies used in NLP. This is what we're asking you to do now that you've done both of those things. We want you to take the NLP knowledge you already have and apply it to the situations you face on a daily basis. Therefore, the purpose of this brief but informative chapter is to offer some basic but extremely useful recommendations on how you might effectively, efficiently, and successfully apply the three primary NLP tools and strategies that you've learnt to your day-to-day life.

You have dedicated a significant portion of your time to gaining knowledge on how to use NLP techniques to achieve success through a step-by-step process known as the Well-Formed Outcome, how you can influence other people through communication techniques, and how you can easily gain confidence through the NLP technique known as anchoring. In addition, you have spent some time learning how to use NLP techniques to communicate effectively with others. You should have ideally picked up a lot of information even if this book is on the shorter side. Because of this, we want to make sure that the implementation of the NLP tools and approaches that you choose goes off without a hitch. We suggest putting your NLP skills to use in chunks in order to get the greatest results with this. That is, do not go to work tomorrow with the intention of putting into practise all of the strategies that have been discussed in this book in a single day. Instead, you should think about implementing the Well-Formed Outcome over the course of two weeks. Then, during the third week, you should use your NLP influencing abilities, and during the fourth week, you should practise creating anchors and employ them. The application of your understanding of NLP should thus take the form of something like this:

Weeks 1 and 2 Put everything you've studied in Chapter 2 -- Achieving Success -- to use during this application week. Our accomplishments are a direct result of the goals we have set for ourselves, therefore the first thing you should do is decide what it is you want to do. It is not necessary for this to be an insane or protracted endeavour. In point of fact, we strongly recommend that you begin on a modest scale. Consider a target that can be completed in the span of a single whole week. Consider that you would want to reduce the amount of time you spend on social media during your lunch break. Apply each stage of the Well-Formed Outcome process that we covered after you have determined what you want to accomplish. Utilise the worksheet that we have supplied for you, and devote the whole of this week to making headway towards achieving your objective. After you have successfully completed your goal within one full week's time, you should set a new, somewhat more ambitious objective for yourself and allow yourself an additional week and a half to complete it. Make the process of goal-setting a regular part of your routine, whether it be weekly or monthly, but be sure to give yourself objectives that are both relevant and attainable on a regular basis.

Week 3: In addition to creating goals using NLP's Well-Formed Outcome, you should now also focus on applying NLP's influencing strategies to your professional or personal endeavours. These techniques may be used to either your career or personal life. You should spend some time each morning this week reading through the NLP influencing tactics covered in Chapter 3, deciding which technique you are going to put into practise and use, and then really using that technique. You don't want to overload yourself (or others, for that matter), so stick to employing just one approach each day until you feel comfortable adding others. On the first day of the event, you should make an effort to shake hands with someone you've just met or spoken to in order to demonstrate that you have a genuine interest in them and that you have enjoyed talking to them about their ideas. After you've had a conversation with someone on Day Two about an issue that's significant to both of you, make an effort to develop a connection with them by quickly patting or laying your hand on their shoulder. Maintain this routine throughout the remainder of the week in a consistent manner. Experiment over the course of the next several weeks with using many strategies in a single day or with employing multiple strategies on various persons that you intend to influence.

Week 4: On the first day of this week, devote your time to reviewing the material included in Chapter 4 about the development of a confidence anchor via the use of NLP strategies. The second day should be devoted to practising and developing a confidence anchor for yourself. If you have a lot of success with this, you should consider what additional qualities or feelings you would want to anchor and then follow the methods outlined in Chapter 4 to do so in the right order. You should have many productive anchors at the end of the week that you are able to readily rely upon at any given point. This should be the case. Keep in mind that it's important to reset your moorings on a regular basis.

The Fact That Others Control And Dominate Them Is The Utmost Reality Of The Situation

Every single idea, characteristic, and behavioural attribute of psychopathy that we have covered in this article can probably be summed up in one: the uncanny need of psychopaths to subjugate others by controlling and dominating them. Psychopaths do not see other people as human beings who can be engaged in conversation on an equal footing. They see people as instruments that can be studied, comprehended, exploited, manipulated, dominated, and controlled. They see human vulnerability in the same way that a tradesman views the handle of the tool he uses for his trade, and the more experience they have in using this tool, the more effectively they are able to manipulate vulnerable people. This kind of psychopathy is shown in a benign and maybe more moderate form by successful business leaders in the form known as fearless dominance. These leaders are characterised by an extreme lack of fear.

MACHIAVELLIANIST VIEWPOINT

If you are familiar with the history of politics in Europe, the term "Machiavellianism" is likely to bring to mind the name of Niccol Machiavelli (1469-1527), the author of the book "The Prince," who is considered to be one of the most renowned and notorious political philosophers of the Renaissance period. The Prince, which is still widely read as a political work today, albeit hopefully more out of curiosity than for the sake of learning the abhorrent things it teaches, is one text that has maintained its popularity.

NiccoloMachiavelliwrote, "A wise ruler should never keep faith when doing so would be against his interest," as the saying goes. "It would be against his interest." He also said, "A Prince never lacks good reason to break his promise," which is one of his most famous quotes. According to Niccolo Machiavelli, honesty and other humane qualities might be done away with if deceit, treachery, and force would be more useful as a means to a goal. In other words, honesty and other humane virtues can be rendered obsolete. Niccolo Machiavelli made the argument that rulers may readily embrace this style of governing even if it might not be their natural style of ruling, but because it would be more effective in doing so. He said this despite the fact that it might not be the rulers' natural style of ruling.

A SUMMARY OF THE HISTORY OF POLITICAL MACHEVELLIANISM

In 1912, Niccolo Machiavelli was forced out of Italy's political life and exiled from the country. After that, he devoted his life to writing, and during the course of his career, he produced a great number of works, the most well-known of which is his book. The Prince, which was destined to become a famous book due to its objectionable themes and advice on leadership, which come off as being entirely objectionable, was destined to become famous. The book encourages the idea that those in positions of authority should strive to behave in the most conscientious manner possible. Some of these methods include resorting to deceit, treachery, the elimination of political opponents, and the use of fear as a means of exerting control over the people being manipulated. It is generally accepted that the most important part of what Machiavelli says in the book of his is the proposition that establishing a state and maintaining it requires effort in the afterlife. Machiavellian is an adjective that is used to characterise a kind of politics that is characterised by cunning, being two-faced, treachery, and is destined to end badly because of Machiavelli's advice. This advice helped make Machiavelli famous.

Because of his book, Niccolo Machiavelli gained a significant amount of notoriety. The Prince, but apart from that, there is also his other major work, The Course on Livy, which is a book on how to construct a republican state and h's advice on how to keep it orderly. The Course on Livy is a book on how to keep it orderly. He made the observation that free republics had an advantageous power structure in comparison to principalities. He also discussed the benefits of having a republican government as opposed to a monarchical one in another part of his speech. It should be noted that the author's other works include several examples of his controversial comments. One of those well-known and much debated assertions is that, on occasion, violent means may be necessary in order to restore order in a corrupt city. He also praised the ancient Roman ruler Romulus for killing his own brother and fellow ruler in order to have authority solely to himself in order to construct the city of Rome. This was done so that Romulus could establish Rome as the only ruler. In a couple of other sections, he acted out the part of a counsellor to a tyrant as well. Scholars have observed that the philosophical foundations on which Niccolo's views on principalities and his deal republic are built are not that unlike to one another. This is due to the fact that both of these political systems rely on quite ruthless methods for aggrandisement and empire building.

In one of the sections, Machiavelli argues against Cicero's recommendation that they steer clear of violence and duplicity. Machiavelli said in this passage that the prince "should be the fox to avoid the snares and the lion to overwhelm the wolve." This has become one of his most famous statements during the course of his career.

It has been discovered that cruelty and murder both play such an important part in his politics. This explains, in large part, why related topics like murder and betrayal often come up throughout the course of the story. It has been discovered that Machiavelli's own definition of virtue is unique in that it is distinct and more dynamic in comparison to the concepts of other political philosophers. He gave his own brand of virtue the name virtu. According to him, the only time virtue is useful is when it assists a ruler in maintaining their state. As a result, it is essential that he be willing to engage in necessary evil when it would be to his own profit.

Because the book presented such a controversial viewpoint on political issues, in 1559, the Catholic church decided to put a ban on The Prince. In addition to that, the book was added to the index known as the librorumprohibitorum.

Another thing that Machiavelli criticised and rejected was the traditional Christian and Jewish teachings. In his opinion, these teachings rendered the Italians of his day feeble and effeminate since they celebrated humility and otherworldly things. It is generally accepted that Niccolo Machiavelli had a dim view of the Christianity practised in the modern era.

Developing become a skilled facilitator

In addition to having extensive information on the topic at hand, facilitators are expected to have a pleasant attitude and be accessible. It's not good for the growth of a team to have members that are frightening. An atmosphere that is open to learning may be fostered by a facilitator who encourages participants to share their own perspectives. Aside from that, facilitators have a responsibility to provide assistance. The quality of the conversation may be significantly enhanced by providing a reluctant participant with positive reinforcement in the form of encouragement to express their thoughts. People that have ideas that are beneficial will often give them some consideration before sharing them with others.

The Psychology Behind The Game Of Manipulation Recognizing The Craft Of Manipulation And The Skills Necessary To Evaluate People

What exactly do we mean when we refer to the "psychology of manipulation," and what exactly do we mean by that phrase? Enticing another person to act in a certain way against their will is an example of manipulation. A lot of individuals often get manipulation and deceit mixed up in their heads. To clear the air then, what exactly is meant by the term "deception"? A person may manipulate another person via deception, which is also an art form. When someone deceives another person into doing anything, the outcome is almost never positive. awareness these two requires a clear awareness of their differences. In addition to this, it paints a detailed picture of how both of these things operate on a person or group of individuals.

Manipulation occurs all the time and every day in a variety of social circles, including the classroom, the family (most often carried out by siblings), and even the business (carried out either by coworkers or even by managers). The question now is, what exactly is the psychology behind manipulation? Manipulation is the process of influencing another person's thoughts by intervening in their mental processes in order to get them to carry out the desired action of the manipulator. The person who manipulates others is referred to as the manipulator, and the one who is manipulated is the person who is asked to do something by the manipulator. Because the manipulator always has the upper hand in the issue or topic, manipulation is an activity that always goes in one direction.

Blackmail is another kind of manipulation that may be used. When a manipulator does this, they are using the person they are manipulating's vulnerabilities or dirty little secrets to persuade them to do something for them. The majority of the time, manipulation is a sleazy game that is played by others in order to further their own interests. One side of a manipulative situation will almost always have a good time with it, and that side is, of course, the side that comes out on top in the end. People who engage in manipulative behaviour believe that life is a game of give and take. They also think that manipulation is a simple and quick approach to have all of their wants and desires met at the same time.

It is a game for some individuals most of the time, particularly in youngsters, and this holds true the majority of the time. They are well aware of the detrimental consequences it has on their lives. Their primary objective is to just play and enjoy themselves as much as possible before they reach an age when games become tedious. The manipulation of older individuals is more severe, and it often results in the older person getting what they want in an easy and expedient manner. Therefore, manipulation is more about persuading someone to do what you want them to do without considering other people, which is incredibly selfish. In both directions, manipulation has more of a physical and psychological component. Throughout the whole of this sadistic game, it serves to both delight the manipulator and maintain the manipulated person in a state of humiliation at the hands of the manipulator.

In addition to this, the book discusses the psychology behind manipulating individuals and many methods for characterising them. Both the practise of manipulation as an art and the ways in which individuals put it to use are topics that are covered in this particular subject or chapter. The technique of convincing individuals to act in accordance with one's desires is known as manipulation. This chapter discusses all there is to know about manipulating others. One of the other parts of this chapter focuses on the ways in which manipulation may be utilised to analyse individuals. This is the psychological chapter that discusses persons playing mind games with others, as well as the question of whether or not this individual is capable of being evaluated by psychiatrists.

Then, what exactly is the psychology behind manipulating others? Understanding both the skill of manipulation and the motivations behind it are essential components of the psychology of manipulation. The concept of manipulation has already been discussed, yet one may wonder why individuals tempt or coerce others to behave what they want. People who are good at manipulating others have a lot of joy getting people to act in the way they want them to. They take pleasure in both tormenting those who are easily persuaded and achieving their goals. At other situations, manipulation can even be considered a form of psychological torture. If nothing is done to remedy the situation, it's possible that someone might sustain injuries, whether they be physical, mental, or even psychological. The failure to rein in manipulative behaviour might result in catastrophic and in some cases irreparable repercussions.

The study of manipulation's psychological effects reveals that the practise is, in some ways, similar to bullying, which results in a psychologically tormented conscience. The activities that one is expected to accomplish are designed to induce one to experience discomfort, whether it psychological or bodily. They keep the people who are being controlled on their toes by instilling in them a persistent worry that they may be asked to do another assignment in the near future. They may make a person terrified and exceedingly suspicious of everyone in their immediate environment. The majority of these activities that people are required to undertake leave permanent scars and make these individuals very susceptible. The manipulators need to be warned, and their victims ought to be kept at arm's length from one other, if the manipulated are not to face an even greater psychological uphill battle.

Most of the time, manipulating other people begins as a game that individuals play in order to feel better about themselves. When things start to go more smoothly in the game, one of the manipulators will keep doing his goofy and childish things to try to win. The more he or she engages in these nasty mind games, the more fun and invested he or she will get in them. These mental games keep the other party in the dark and ensnare them in all the excitement, which is a kind of torment and a living nightmare for them. The manipulator will eventually do it on a daily basis just for their own entertainment until it becomes a habit.

People almost always perceive manipulation to be a game in their minds. It is far more than that, and it is a much more hazardous technique to punish people: physically, intellectually, and most crucially, psychologically. People who are subjected to torture run the risk of developing psychological stress disorders if the situation is not properly addressed and remedied. Depending on the individual and where they are in relation to the situation, manipulation may either be enjoyable or torturous. There are manipulators in every environment, and everyone of them has their own unique strategy for committing acts of iniquity and immoral behaviour. Manipulation is an inherent element of life and may be found in almost any setting.

The issue of manipulation is one that is fraught with sensitivity, yet it is important that it be discussed. At no point in time should manipulation be disregarded as irrelevant. Everyone should strive towards making things better and removing the concerns of manipulation, and the topic of manipulation should be addressed in big groups in all social institutions such as schools, companies, and homes as well. This is done so that individuals won't engage in such negative and irritating behaviour. In order to prevent other instances of manipulation from occurring, it is imperative that every detriment be outlined. If all of these precautions are taken, the rate of data tampering should drop to a negligible amount or even become completely absent after all of these safeguards are in place.

www.ingramcontent.com/pod-product-compliance
Lightning Source LLC
Chambersburg PA
CBHW050418120526
44590CB00015B/2011